World About Us

Metals

By Sarah Levete

Stargazer Books

Designed and produced by
Aladdin Books Ltd

First published in the
United States in 2006 by
Stargazer Books
c/o The Creative Company
123 South Broad Street
P.O. Box 227
Mankato, Minnesota 56002

Printed in Malaysia

Editor:
Harriet Brown

Designers:
Flick, Book Design and Graphics
Simon Morse

Picture Researcher:
Alexa Brown

Literacy Consultant:
Jackie Holderness—former Senior
Lecturer in Primary Education,
Westminster Institute,
Oxford Brookes University

Library of Congress Cataloging-in-Publication Data

Levete, Sarah.
   Metals / by Sarah Levete.
      p. cm. -- (World about us)
   Includes index.
   ISBN 1-59604-043-2
   1. Metals--Juvenile literature.
   I. Title. II. Series: World
about us (North Mankato,
Minn.)

TN667.L48 2005
669--dc22

                    2005042526

CONTENTS

Notes to parents and teachers

This series has been developed for group use in the classroom, as well as for children reading alone. In particular, its text on two levels allows children of mixed abilities to enjoy reading about the same topic. The larger size text (A, below) offers apprentice readers a simplified text. This simplified text is used in the introduction to each chapter and in the picture captions. This font is part of the © Sassoon family whose maximum legibility is recommended for early readers. The smaller size text (B, below) offers a more challenging read for older or more able readers.

Bend and stretch

Metals are strong, but they can be made into many shapes. There are lots of ways to shape metal.

A

◀ Copper is pulled into thin wires.

Hot metal can be poured into a mold to set, like jello—but the cold metal will not wobble!

B

Questions, key words, and glossary

Each spread ends with a question that parents and teachers can use to discuss and develop further ideas and concepts. Further questions are provided in a quiz on page 30. A reduced version of pages 30 and 31 is shown below. The illustrated "Key words" section is provided as a revision tool, particularly for apprentice readers, in order to help with spelling, writing, and guided reading. The glossary is for more able or older readers.

In addition to the glossary's role as a reference aid, it is also designed to reinforce new vocabulary and provide a tool for further discussion and revision. When glossary terms first appear in the text they are highlighted in bold.

 See how much you know!

Are metals soft or hard?

Can you see through metal?

Where are metals found?

Which metals are precious?

Why is stainless steel used for knives and forks?

Which metal is a liquid at room temperature?

What is a mixture of metals called?

Are metals only found in the ground?

How can you sort different metals?

Key words

Mining

A

Bronze	**Electricity**
Gold	**Geologist**
Iron	**Mercury**

Rust

Glossary

Alloy—A metal mixed with other metals or materials.
Conductor—A material through which electricity can flow.
Extract—To take something out.
Geologists—People who study the earth.
Habitat—The natural homes of plants and animals.
Magma—Hot liquid rock.
Open cast mine—A mine near the surface of the ground.
Ore—Rock that contains metal.
Oxygen—A gas that is all around us.

B

Recycling—To use again and again.
Smelting—Burning rocks to separate out the metal.
Superplastic—A strong, stretchy alloy.
Welding—Using heat to melt and stick things together.

What are metals?

Metals are everywhere! You can see and touch metals in the kitchen, in the street, or at school. Some metals are strong and shiny. Others are thin and bendable. This metal bridge is strong enough to carry lots of heavy cars and trucks.

◀ **This metal boat can push through ice.**

We often say that something is made from metal but there are many different metals. Each one has a special feature that makes it useful for certain jobs. Strong steel is used to make machines and boats. Copper, aluminum, zinc, tin, and lead are some other metals—there are many more!

▶ Metals are hard and solid.

Metals are usually solid and hard. They have a fixed shape. Most metals turn into a runny liquid when heated to very high temperatures. They turn back into a solid shape when they cool down.

Metals are often shiny.

There are many words to describe the feel of metals and what they do. Metal tools do not bend easily. A metal bridge is strong. You can't see through metal. Some metals are shiny and others turn rusty. Some metals feel smooth, and others feel rough. Metals are waterproof.

Musical instrument

Garden tools

Saw

Coin

 How many different metals can you name?

Where metals come from

Most metals are found inside rocks, at the bottom of the sea, and even in the center of the earth. All over the world, there are rocks above the ground and under the ground. Inside these rocks are different types of metals.

◀ Hot, runny metals ooze out of this volcano.

It takes thousands of years for metals to form under the ground. Hot liquid rock, called **magma,** and other materials mix together. As the mixture cools down, metals form inside rocks. A rock with plenty of metal inside it is called an **ore.** Sometimes the rocks are pushed to the earth's surface by volcanoes.

The map shows you where metals are found.

Metals are found all over the world. Some rocks only contain tiny amounts of metal, but others have large amounts. Digging up rocks is expensive so it is important for **geologists** to know where metals are found.

▲ **Geologists are scientists who study rocks.**

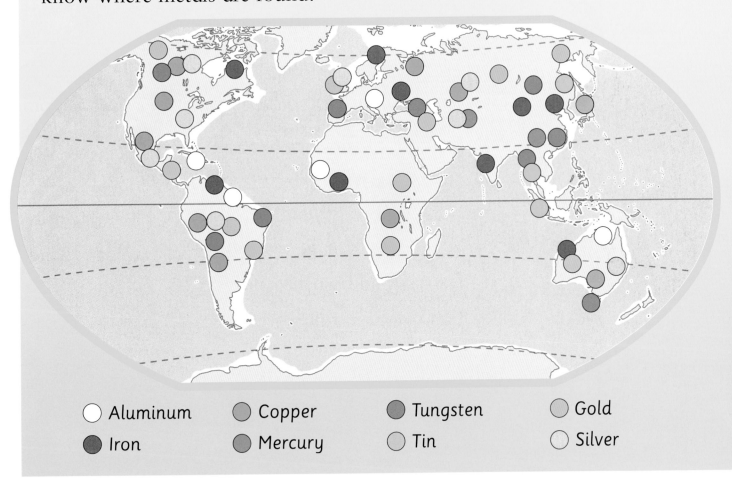

○ Aluminum	○ Copper	○ Tungsten	○ Gold
● Iron	○ Mercury	○ Tin	○ Silver

 What happens when a volcano explodes?

Mining for metals

You can find some metals in rivers or buried at the bottom of the sea. Others, such as iron, are found in rocks deep under the ground. There are many ways to dig rocks out of the ground. This is called mining.

◀ **This is a big mine.**

Have you ever seen a hole in the ground, the size of 1,000 soccer fields? It may be an **open cast mine**, dug by machines and miners. Metals such as copper lie in rocks near the ground. They are dug from these open cast mines. Huge drills and blasts of explosives loosen the rocks. Special machines scoop out the rocks and load them onto trucks.

▶ Digging underground is hard work.

Many miners work deep underground digging for ores. The miners build tunnels that they can move along. With drills, saws, and explosives they cut away the rocks. Deep underground mining is tough work.

Mines can destroy the homes of people, animals, and plants.

Sometimes, people have to move home as whole villages are destroyed so an area can be mined. The **habitats** of animals and plants can be destroyed by mining works. Traffic from the mines can also harm the environment. Mines can spoil the look of the countryside.

 Why do you think some people don't like mines?

Rock to metal

Before we can use metal and make it into useful objects, it must be taken out of the rock. When the rocks have been dug out of the ground, they are taken to a factory. Here, the metal is taken out. This is done in different ways for different kinds of metal.

◄ Rock can be taken to a factory by truck.

Metal ores are loaded onto trucks, ships, and trains to take them from a mine to a factory. This may be in another country. At the factory, the ore goes though many processes, or changes. The metal is **extracted** or taken out of the rock. There are many ways to do this.

◀ Rocks are heated up in huge hot ovens.

Sometimes, the rocks are put into huge ovens called blast furnaces. The rock is heated up to incredibly high temperatures. In the burning heat, the metal is separated from the rock. This process is called **smelting**. It is used to extract iron from its ore.

Electricity is used to take metal out of rocks.

Some metals, such as aluminum, are separated from their ores using electricity. Aluminum ore is mixed with other chemicals. Electricity is passed through it. This is called electrolysis and it separates out the aluminum.

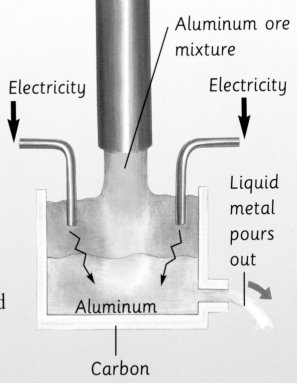

Aluminum ore mixture

Electricity

Electricity

Liquid metal pours out

Aluminum

Carbon

 Can you think of one use for aluminum in your kitchen?

Mixing metals

Some metals can be used on their own. Copper is used to make wires. Metals can also be mixed with other things, to make stronger or more useful metal. A mixture of copper and zinc makes strong and shiny brass.

◀ **Bronze is a mixture of copper and tin.**

A metal that is used on its own is called a pure metal. A metal that is mixed with another material is called an **alloy**. Alloys can have special features to do special jobs. Mixing copper and tin makes bronze. This is stronger than pure tin and it doesn't rust.

▶ Some metals can be made very strong!

There are some alloys called **superplastic** alloys. These are made using a mixture of aluminum and other materials. The mixture is heated up to make the alloy both strong and stretchy. Superplastic alloys are useful in buildings, cars, trains, and airplanes.

Some metals rust when they become wet.

Have you ever seen a rough brown-red patch on a car? This is rust. Iron metal turns rusty when it becomes wet. A few metals, such as gold, never turn rusty. Special paints or coverings can stop a metal such as iron from rusting.

 Why are mixtures of metals useful?

Bend and stretch

Metals are strong, but they can be made into many shapes. There are lots of ways to shape metal. Most metals can be bent and pulled when they are very hot. A few metals, such as copper, lead, and gold, can be shaped even when they are cold.

◀ Copper is pulled into thin wires.

Hot, runny metal can be poured into a mold to set, like jello—but the cold metal will not wobble! Hot steel is squashed in huge rollers. Gold and silver can be hammered into sheets as thin as paper. Copper is stretched into thin tube shapes to be used for wires. Copper and gold do not have to be heated before they are shaped.

Hot metal glues two pieces of metal together.

A car is made out of many pieces of metal. These are joined together by **welding**. A special hot flame melts the edges of two pieces of metal. Hot, runny metal glues them together.

The thin part in this bulb is metal!

Can you see the very thin wire inside this light bulb? This is made out of the metal tungsten. It glows brightly when hot and it does not melt. This piece of tungsten is longer than a grown man but it is so thin it can be wound up into this tiny space.

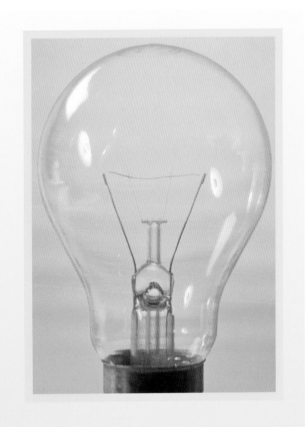

 What happens to most metals when they get very hot?

17

Important iron

The center of the earth is partly made of iron! Around the world, there is plenty of iron found in rocks. Some of the rocks look rusty and red. When the iron is taken out, it is dark gray. Iron is a useful and important metal.

◀ **Iron is strong and easy to shape.**

In its ore, iron is mixed with many other materials. To extract the iron, the rocks are heated in extremely hot ovens, called blast furnaces. When other materials, such as coke and limestone, are added, runny iron is extracted. The purest iron is then used to make steel.

◀ This ship is made from strong steel.

Iron cracks easily and rusts if it becomes wet. Steel is stronger and easier to shape. To make steel, hot iron is mixed with the gas oxygen. Stainless steel is used for cutlery because it doesn't rust.

Iron has always been an important metal.

Blowing air onto a fire makes it very hot. When a piece of rock containing iron is heated this way in a charcoal fire, you end up with a lump of iron! This discovery, about 3,000 years ago, began the period of history we call the Iron Age.

Iron armor

Iron weapons

 How many things made of iron or steel can you name?

Light and strong

Many metals, such as iron and steel, are strong and heavy. They are used to make machines or buildings. There is also a need for metals that are strong and light. A car needs to be strong, but it uses up less gas if it is also light.

◀ Aircraft need to be strong and light.

A light aircraft is cheaper to fly than a heavy one because it uses less fuel. It is also faster. But aircraft must be strong too. Titanium is as strong as steel but nearly half as light! This airplane is made mainly out of the metals titanium and aluminum.

This metal was worth more than gold!

Aluminum used to be more valuable than gold! It was precious because it was hard to find and costly to make. Today, it is much cheaper and is used to make cans and kitchen foil.

There is metal in your body.

Inside your body, there are tiny natural traces of metal such as iron and zinc. These are not chunks of solid iron. Instead, these metals flow around your body in your blood. Metals in the body are called minerals. We get them from eating different foods.

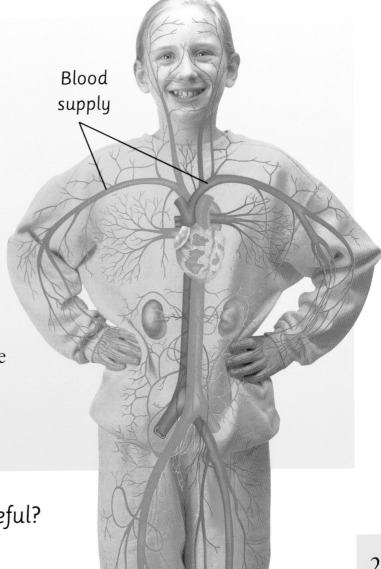

Blood supply

 Why are light metals useful?

Useful metals

You can see and touch metals used in things like drink cans and bicycles. Metals also make it possible for you to switch on a light. Your computer uses metals to work and there is even metal in the paint on your walls.

◀ **Electricity flows easily through some metals.**

Electricity only flows easily through some materials. It cannot flow through wood or plastic. But it can flow through some metals, such as copper. These metals are called **conductors**. Many electrical wires are made from copper. Without metals, we could not use electricity as we do today.

What would happen if you had a wooden saucepan?

Many materials catch fire easily. A wooden saucepan would burn if it was heated. A metal saucepan gets hot but does not melt. Metal is a good conductor of heat. It lets heat through, but doesn't burn unless it is extremely hot.

Mercury is a runny metal.

Mercury is the only metal that stays as a liquid at room temperature. This silver-colored metal used to be called quicksilver because of the way it runs and flows. Mercury changes shape when it heats up or cools down. Because of this it can be used in thermometers to measure temperature.

 Can you think of ten things that we need metals for?

Shiny and gold!

Gold, silver, and platinum are special metals. They are used to make necklaces and bracelets. These metals cost a lot of money because they are hard to find. Precious metals are very important because they have other uses—they are even used in space.

◀ **Gold was once used as money.**

Rare metals are often called precious metals. They are worth a lot of money. Gold is only found in a few rocks, although in some parts of the world, you may be lucky and find a nugget of gold in some river mud! Gold and silver sparkle and shine. Platinum is a beautiful silver-white color. It is very tough.

◄ Gold is not just for looking good!

Precious metals are not just used for jewelry. Platinum can stand the highest temperatures. Gold reflects heat and light. It is used on spacecraft to protect them from the sun. Silver conducts electricity and is used in making photographs.

Polishing silver keeps it shiny!

Metals can look shiny, and they can look dull. Most metals need polishing to stay shiny. This is because the gas called oxygen mixes with the metal and makes it look dull. Polishing a metal returns its shiny look.

Polished silver ring

Tarnished silver trophy

 Why is gold expensive and iron cheap?

Old to new

Much of the metal we use has been used before. You can use metals again and again, by melting them down and making new things from them. This is called recycling. Recycling is very important.

◀ **Recycling saves energy.**

Taking metal from rocks in the ground is expensive and uses up lots of energy. It creates **pollution** when the rocks are shipped across the world in trucks and boats. Each year, we use so many aluminum cans that if you stacked them, they could reach to the moon and back! You can make twenty **recycled** cans with the same energy needed to make just one new can.

▶ A magnet sorts out different metals.

Machines chew up the old bits of metal in washing machines, cars, and cans. The machine squeezes out small clean pieces of metal. A huge magnet separates iron and steel. Each type of metal is melted down and used again.

Steel can

Aluminum can

Paper clip

Copper coin

Silver coin

Gold ring

You can sort out different metals.

Some metals are magnetic. This means they will be pulled toward a magnet. Iron and steel are magnetic. Copper and brass are not. With a small magnet, try to pick up a selection of metal objects. Which ones are magnetic?

? Why is it important to separate different types of metal?

Metals in the future

We use metals every day. Our lives would be very different without metals. Scientists are always finding amazing new ways to use metals. They look for new places to dig for metals and for new metal materials to make.

◀ **There are metals at the bottom of the sea!**

It is expensive to dig deep below the sea but it may cause less pollution and damage to the area than mining on land. Some scientists are looking into ways of using tiny creatures called bacteria to collect the metals from the sea!

◀ Metal blankets keep out flames.

Using aluminum and other metals in blankets keeps in heat and keeps out flames. These thermal blankets are used in space to keep astronauts warm, and here on Earth to protect climbers on cold, snowy mountains.

There are metals in space!

High above the sky, metals are found in shining stars, on other planets, and in huge pieces of rock that float around in space. If humans ever build on another planet, maybe they could use the supply of metal from outer space.

 What would the world be like without metals?

See how much you know!

Are metals soft or hard?

Can you see through metal?

Where are metals found?

Which metals are precious?

Why is stainless steel used for knives and forks?

Which metal is a liquid at room temperature?

What is a mixture of metals called?

Are metals only found in the ground?

How can you sort different metals?

Key words

Mining   **Mine**

Bronze   **Electricity**

Gold   **Geologist**

Iron   **Mercury**

Ore   **Recycling**

Rock   **Silver**

Rust

Glossary

Alloy—A metal mixed with other metals or materials.

Conductor—A material through which electricity can flow.

Extract—To take something out.

Geologists—People who study the earth and the rocks that form it.

Habitat—The natural homes of plants and animals.

Magma—Hot, liquid rock.

Open cast mine—A mine near the surface of the ground.

Ore—Rock that contains metal.

Pollution—Gases, chemicals, or garbage that damage the environment.

Recycling—To use again and again.

Smelting—Burning rocks to separate out the metal.

Superplastic—A strong, stretchy alloy.

Welding—Using heat to melt and stick metal together.

Index

Photocredits:
Abbreviations: l-left, r-right, b-bottom, t-top, c-center, m-middle
Front cover — Flat Earth. Back cover — Photodisc. 11t, 31t — Atlas Copco. 11b — Constock. 3cbl, 3bl, 4b, 5cl, 8b, 15b, 15t, 16b, 19t, 20t, 20b, 22b, 28t, 29b, 30c, 31b — Corbis. 7t, 23t, 24b, 25bl — Corel. 1, 2-3, 3tl, 4t, 5tl, 5tr, 5br, 12b, 13t, 16t, 17t, 18b, 21t, 30t — Flat Earth. 28b — John Harvey. 7cl, 7cr, 7bl, 7cbr, 14t, 17b, 23b, 25bl — Ingram Publishing. 10t, 24t — Johnson Matthey. 26t — Simon Morse. 29t — Outokumpu Technology. 3ctl, 5bl, 6t, 6b, 8t, 10b, 14b, 26b, 27b, 30b — Photodisc. 12t, 21b — Select Pictures. 22t — Rexam. 9t — US Geological Service.